Reading and Writing

Rhona Whiteford

Rhona Whiteford has many years' experience of teaching at preschool and primary school level, and is the author of a wide range of educational books for teachers, parents and children. She has two children.

Consultant: **Andrew Burrell**

Andrew Burrell has worked as a primary school teacher and as a lecturer at the Institute of Education, University of London, and has carried out research into the teaching of Language and Literacy.

Illustrated by **Mike Gibbie**

About this book

This book contains reading and writing activities suitable for 10- and 11-year-olds. They are based on the National Curriculum and National Literacy Strategy requirements for Year 6.

The activities gradually become more demanding, so it is important to start at the beginning.

The reading and writing skills taught or practised in each unit are stated at the top of the page. A note at the foot of the page tells you more about the purpose of the activities and gives advice about how to help your child with them.

Stickers are provided as a reward and as a record, and the progress chart at the back of the book gives you a useful checklist of skills.

Each unit ends with a positive comment. Encouragement from you will work wonders, so be generous with your praise!

How to help your child

- Encourage your child to find a quiet place to work, preferably sitting at a table. This will help concentration.
- Discuss your child's work on a regular basis to maintain interest and motivation.
- Make sure your child has access to good-quality writing materials.
- If possible, buy your child a junior dictionary and a thesaurus. Looking at words helps with spelling skills.
- Play Scrabble and other word games and have fun with spelling quizzes.
- Encourage your child to take responsibility for checking his or her work.

Above all, be relaxed – and have fun!

Hodder Children's Books
a division of
Hodder Headline Limited

A reading questionnaire

I'm Finn, and I'm here to help you with your reading and writing.

1 Answer all the questions, and then review your answer to the first question.

Do you like reading? ....

Do you have reading materials in your home? ....

Do you have books of your own? ....

Do you read for fun? ....

Do you read to find information? ....

Do you go to the library? ....

What do you do there? (✓ or ✗)

Borrow fiction books ☐

Listen to stories ☐

Use the computer ☐

Use the Internet ☐

How often do you buy comics or magazines? (✓ or ✗)

Daily ☐

Weekly ☐

Monthly ☐

How often do you read? (✓ or ✗)

Never, if you can help it ☐

A little each day ☐

About 1 hour each day ☐

About 2 hours each day ☐

Whenever you can ☐

2 Who reads what in your home?

	You	Other family members
Fiction books		
Non-fiction books		
Comics		
Magazines		
Newspapers		
Computer programs		
Internet material		
Letters		
Other		

This questionnaire has been designed to make your child think about what he likes reading. Encourage him to be adventurous when he is choosing books, trying a variety of reading material.

Fiction

◻/10

3 Do you like fiction or non-fiction? Give each a mark out of ten.

Non-fiction

◻/10

4 Colour the squares to give each kind of book a mark out of ten.

Fiction

Adventure	
Fantasy	
History	
Animals	
Comedy	
Legends	
Folk tales	
Science fiction	
Poetry	
School stories	

Non-fiction

Animals	
Nature	
Computing	
Science	
Technology	
History	
Sports	
Crafts	
Art	
Vehicles	

5 What/who is your favourite:

● non-fiction subject?..............................

● fiction genre? ....

● fiction author? ....

● person to read you a story? ....

● place to read quietly? ....

● story tape? ....

● fiction book?

....

● non-fiction book?

....

6 Do you really like reading?

Yes ◻ No ◻

Discuss the reading tastes of other family members. Make sure that your child understands the difference between someone's opinion of a book (e.g. *I thought this book was very exciting*), and a fact (e.g. *This book is about a family of foxes*).

Thoughtful! ★

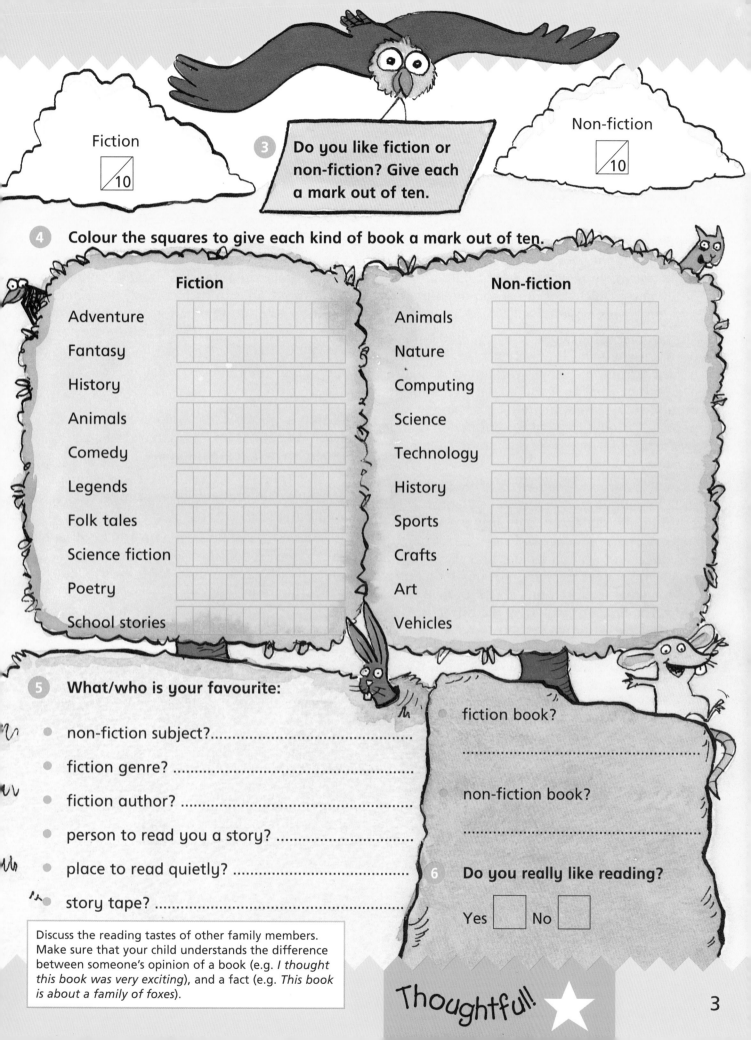

Reading carefully

Read this passage from *Dolphin Luck* by Hilary McKay, and then answer the questions.

"No, I don't!" said Mr. Robinson, and stamped off to shut himself in the kitchen to finish preparing dinner. He was the sort of man who could not cook unless he had absolute privacy and silence, which, Mrs. Robinson sometimes remarked, was all very well.

"If that dog comes back," he promised himself as he turned down the oven to give the turkey a final browning, "I shall wait until the children are back at school …" (He added cream to the bread sauce, stirred it carefully, ground in black pepper, tasted it, paused to consider, and added two drops of lemon juice and an invisible quantity of salt.)

"Yes, I'll wait until they are at school and then I shall telephone that vet myself … (Those potatoes are done, and the sprouts. Another sixty seconds, perhaps, for utter perfection) … explain about his bad temper and the dreadful smell, which does exist, it is not my imagination whatever the children say … (That gravy is perfect, a bay leaf makes all the difference) … After all, he is fourteen at least and possibly more … (That sauce could be warmer and the gravy should always be boiling hot. It is a well known fact that all the best cooks are men. Attention to detail and absolutely critical timing, that's what it comes down to. Colander!) … Yes, I shall explain about his age … (Colander, colander, colander, it's vanished) … and suggest that it would be doing the dog a kindness … What on earth is that terrible stench?"

It was more than a year since Old Blanket had been thin enough to squeeze through the enormous catflap that had been cut for him in the kitchen door, but he appeared to have forgotten this fact.

"It simply isn't fair," moaned Mr. Robinson. Old Blanket was sodden and snarling and appeared to have swollen to twice his usual size. It took Perry and his father more than half an hour to extract him from the kitchen door, the whole operation having to be performed from behind in the rain, because of his ominous growls throughout the rescue.

"Poor, poor darling!" said Ant.

"He smells a bit," said Perry.

"He smells an awful lot," said Beany, who always told the truth. "He's been rolling in washed-up dead seagulls again."

"He eats them, too," remarked Sun Dance, "so I think Old Blanket is very brave. When is it dinner time?"

Mr. Robinson, who had been quietly beating his head against the kitchen wall, suddenly stiffened and made a dash for the stove, but his wife got there before him.

"You can't possibly touch anything until you've had a bath," she ordered her husband as she steered him out of the kitchen, "and neither can Perry! You're both covered in … in … well, whatever Old Blanket's been rolling in!"

"Seagulls," said Beany.

"I can't believe it's just seagulls! Ant, don't you dare go near that dog! Put some sausages in his dish and put him out in the porch, he will have to be scrubbed but I can't face it at the moment. Beany, get your father a drink. Whisky. He won't want anything in it. Take it up to him, Sun Dance, and tell him I am rescuing the dinner …"

Read the passage aloud to give your child a sense of the characters and the humour. Read the questions, and then read the passage again, asking your child to keep the questions in her mind. Encourage her to look back at the text when she is answering the questions, finding evidence to support her answers.

1. Who is Mr. Robinson talking to as he cooks?
Give two quotations from the passage to support your answer.

....

....

2. What is Mr. Robinson really concentrating on, and how do you know this?

....

3. Which verb tenses are used in his speech?

....

....

4. What does **doing the dog a kindness** mean?

....

....

5. What are Mr. Robinson and Perry doing behind Old Blanket in the rain?

....

....

....

6. What makes Mr. Robinson remember his cooking?

....

....

7. What does Mr. Robinson do that shows he is frustrated?

....

....

8. Name one thing that Mrs. Robinson does to sort out the situation.

....

....

9. What do you think happens next?

....

....

See page 6 to find out!

This is how Hilary McKay ended the episode.
Read it carefully, and then answer the questions.

Despite Mrs. Robinson's valiant efforts, dinner was beyond rescue. The turkey had browned to a point that could only be described as black, the bread sauce and gravy had turned to glue and the vegetables boiled to soup. And when dinner was over, the dreadful ordeal of scrubbing Old Blanket had to be faced. It was done in the garden with a hosepipe and a bucketful of dog shampoo. Mr. Robinson was restrained with difficulty from using bleach.

After Old Blanket had been scrubbed, he was shut in the kitchen to dry. While he was there he ate the whole of the remains of the turkey and a box of rum truffles.

On Boxing Day morning he bit Mr. Robinson for no apparent reason, unless it was true, as Ant said defensively, that he sensed Mr. Robinson had stopped loving him.

On Boxing Day afternoon he crawled under Mr. and Mrs. Robinson's bed and was terribly sick. "Food poisoning," said Ant, scowling at her father's bandaged hand.

On Boxing Day evening he died.

From *Dolphin Luck* by Hilary McKay

10 The final five paragraphs are short and snappy.
Why do you think the author wrote them like this?

....

....

11 What feelings did you have as you read this extract?

....

12 Is this how you thought things would turn out?

....

....

13 Do you like this style of writing?

....

14 Do you want to read the rest of the book?

....

Discuss features of the writing in this story – the theme, the style, the characters. Discuss your reactions to the death of Old Blanket. Does the humour make it more or less sad?

6

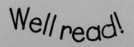

What do you think?

Thinking is hard work!

1 Do you have a favourite author?
Why do you like his or her writing?
Think about these features before you answer.

Form
prose
poetry
comic strip
playscript

Style
strong energetic serious
gentle funny exciting
descriptive

Vocabulary
simple clear varied
unusual archaic
modern slang

Characters
animal human (child, adult)
alien fantasy good bad funny

Genre (type of story)
romance fairy tale fantasy
science fiction history animal story
comedy legend adventure

....

....

....

2 Take notes to compare two authors.

Helen Cresswell ... *David Almond*

Lucy Daniels ... *C.S. Lewis* ... *Anne Fine*

Name	Name
A book title	A book title
Genre	Genre
Form	Form
Style	Style
Characters	Characters
Vocabulary	Vocabulary

J.K. Rowling   Dick King-Smith   Jenny Oldfield   Michael Morpurgo

Discuss your child's favourite fiction authors, encouraging
him to answer Question 1 in complete sentences.
Your own observations will serve as a model for his.

Brilliant!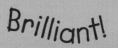

7

Be a playwright!

Every action is written down.

DIRECTOR

1 **Continue this poem in playscript form.**
Think about these features of a playscript.

Characters' names are written on the left-hand side.

There are no speech marks.

Information for actors (prompts) are written in brackets after the character's name.

Stage directions (where things are, what happens and how) can be written in a different style.

Blame

Graham, look at Maureen's leg,
She says you tried to tattoo it!
I did, Miss, yes – with my biro,
But Jonathan told me to do it.

Graham, look at Peter's sock,
It's got a burn-hole through it!
It was just an experiment, Miss,
*   with the lens,*
Jonathan told me to do it.

Alice's bag is stuck to the floor,
Look, Graham, did you glue it?
Yes, but I never thought it would work,
Jonathan told me to do it.

Jonathan, what's all this I hear
About you and Graham Prewitt?
Well, Miss, it's really more his fault:
He tells me to tell him to do it!

By Allan Ahlberg

Scene: *School classroom Teacher talking to one boy at the front of the class*
Children silent

Teacher: (*crossing arms, looking stern*)
Graham, look at Maureen's leg. She says you tried to tattoo it!

Graham: (*at front of class, looking relaxed*) I did, Miss, yes – with my biro,
but Jonathan told me to do it.

Teacher: ....

Graham: ....

....

....

....

....

8

Read the poem aloud together, each taking a part and speaking in a suitable voice. Discuss how the text could be dramatised with scenery and actions.

Where are they? How do they speak?

2 Read this passage.

Then choose half of it, and write it in playscript form.

She grinned when she walked into the room.
"There you are! I've been looking everywhere for you guys!"

"Shhhh!" I hissed desperately. "Smorkus Flinders is on the loose.
You don't want him to hear you!"

She laughed. "Oh, don't worry about that turkey!"

"What do you mean?" asked Grakker.

Elspeth waved her hands as if the monster was a minor detail.
"I put him in suspended animation about twenty minutes ago."

We stared at her in astonishment.

Elspeth smiled. "I bet you'd like me to let you loose, wouldn't you?"

"Like it?" roared Grakker. "I order you to free us instantly."

"You could order me if I was a member of the Galactic Patrol," said Elspeth.
"But you told me I couldn't join. So you don't get to give me orders."

I thought Grakker's eyes were going to bulge right out of his head.
"Undo these rings this instant!"

"They're probably too complicated for me. After all, I'm just a little girl."

From *Aliens Stole My Dad* by Bruce Coville

....

....

....

....

....

....

....

Discuss the way in which a character's actions and
mood are revealed through dialogue, and formulate
some prompts (e.g. for Grakker: *struggling inside a
force field*).

To help your child to organise the playscript, let her
underline the characters' names in different colours.

Fantastic!

9

Writing stories

Always plan your writing.
Planning helps you to:
- **think clearly**
- **work quickly**
- **achieve a good result**

Letters, reports and non-fiction writing should all be planned.

Here are some ways of planning your writing.

The spider

Write your main idea on the spider's body.
Jot down the names of people, places and things which are connected with it next to the legs.

Ideas Bank
money reward faithful horse
police computer mobile phone
market place river helicopter
school playground dark cave
mountain

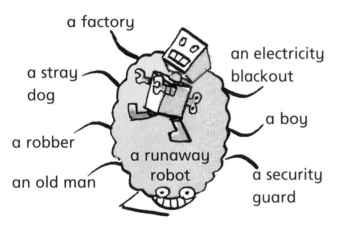

a factory
a stray dog
a robber
an old man
an electricity blackout
a boy
a security guard
a runaway robot

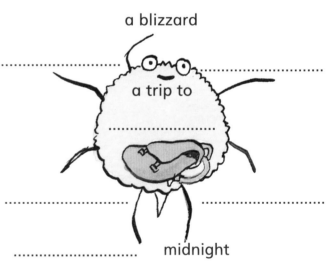

a blizzard
a trip to
midnight

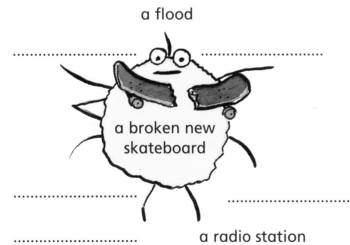

a flood
a broken new skateboard
a radio station

You've made a web site!

This story planning device is useful if you want to brainstorm some ideas together. Encourage your child to jot down random ideas quickly, and then to think of links which could be made between them.

The chain

Write down a main idea or character, concentrate on it, and then write down an idea which is related to the first one. Complete the chain.

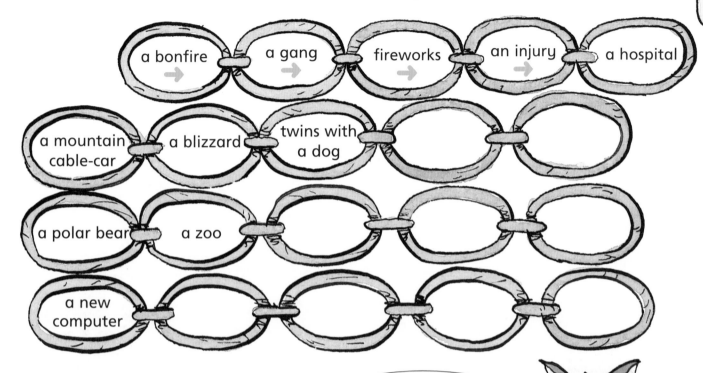

a bonfire → a gang → fireworks → an injury → a hospital

a mountain cable-car — a blizzard — twins with a dog

a polar bear — a zoo

a new computer

The list

Add five ideas to each list.

Work really quickly!

Characters	Events	Feelings
an alien child	a robbery	love
an astronaut	the discovery of a spaceship	hate
a small green talking lizard	lost in a cave	friendship
a sports star	alone inside a computer	greed
....	....	....
....	....	....
....	....	....
....	....	....
....	....	....

The chain device allows your child to develop linked ideas, serious or silly, in sequence.

Play the chain game; one person says a word, and the other has to say a word which is related to the first in some way. You can continue this for as long as you like!

The map

Map the relationships between your characters and their setting. Think about feelings as well as actions.

Let your child draw the arrows in pencil so that she can make changes. Encourage her to be creative: the dolphin could be trapped in a net, or it could become an evil robot!

You can put lots of detail on a sheet like this.

The wall

Use headings for different aspects of your story or report.

Note down your ideas.

Time	**Setting**	**Characters**
Midnight, mid-winter	Hong Kong, skyscraper roof	A 9m dinosaur A boy Scientists

Opening
Scientists want boy to give them the dinosaur for research

Main event 1
Flashback to rainforest – dinosaur egg hatches, boy puts it in a sack, it grows, becomes a pet

Main event 2
Dinosaur holds boy in fist, climbs to roof of skyscraper

Ending
They escape in a hot air balloon

Think of a title.

....

Now write your own plan for a story or report.

Time	Setting	Characters

Opening

Main event 1

Main event 2

Ending

Title

A letter of complaint or an enquiry can be planned using this method. Use headings such as *What happened? When? To whom? How? What do I want to happen next?*

13

Remember that a character may need adjectives from both boxes!

Name	Finn Fox
Age	Young
Male/female	Male
Appearance	Stunning, red, furry
Talents	Good with words
Behaviour	Kind, funny, bold

Choose one of your story ideas on pages 10–13, and think about the characters that story would need.
Now plan two of the characters, using the adjectives in the boxes.

Positive
kind decisive gentle quiet funny enthusiastic honest truthful strong bold brave watchful intelligent thoughtful loyal observant clever dignified

Negative
disloyal unkind rough loud boring mean dull wicked careless weak cowardly wary hesitant clownish dishonest unintelligent

A creature   Name

Age

Male/female

Appearance

Talents

Behaviour

A person   Name

Age

Male/female

Appearance

Talents

Behaviour

I wouldn't do that!

Fancy making it look like that!

I'm like that!

Well!

Talk about the meanings of the words *positive* and *negative*. Explain that they are often used subjectively when people are being described, according to a particular point of view. Look at the words used in this activity, and decide together whether you think each one is in the right box.

The story opening sets the scene, and catches the reader's attention.

Now think about how you will begin your story.
A story opening may be based on:

Description
The sun was at its hottest and it scorched the bare sand of the island's tiny beach. The sea, as if weary, barely moved a wave, and not a breath of wind touched the trees. He landed on the unfriendly shore.

Dialogue
"Where are you?" she shrieked, and her voice echoed back in a panic: "… are you, are you?" Then silence, broken every ten seconds by the steady drip of water. "Here I am!" came a tiny voice at her side. "I've been here all the time …"

Action
It was now or never! They dropped everything where it lay and headed for the capsule. Meteors showered them mercilessly as they heaved the doors shut. The engines were roaring …

... or a combination of all three!

Try out some of these styles here.

Style ....

....
....
....
....
....
....

Style ....

....
....
....
....
....
....

Style ....

....
....
....
....
....
....

Let your child choose one of his story openings and continue the story on a sheet of paper.

Look at stories in books and comics together, and compare different styles of story opening. What kind of impact does each style have?

Well done!

Book or film?

I enjoyed the book and the film but they were different.

Has one of your favourite books been turned into a film or a television programme? Write the titles here.

Book ....

Film/programme ....

Number of times you have read the book		Number of times you have seen the film or programme	

Now compare them by thinking about these things.

Setting

Were they set in the same historical period?　Yes ☐　No ☐

Did the places in the film or programme look
 as they were described in the book?　Yes ☐　No ☐

Did the film or programme show you things that were important
 to the plot, such as a special room or a magician's wand?　Yes ☐　No ☐

Characters

Did the film or programme feature the same
characters as the book?　Yes ☐　No ☐

If not, who was different? ....

Did they look as they were described in the book?...

Were any new characters introduced in the film or programme?.............................

Plot

Were the events in the same order in both versions?　Yes ☐　No ☐

Comment ....

Was the film or programme the length you expected?　Yes ☐　No ☐

Were any new episodes introduced in the film or programme?　Yes ☐　No ☐

Comment ....

Try to give your child access to linked books and films, and encourage her to make comparisons.

Feel

The film or programme was as interesting as the book. (✓ or ✗) ☐

The film or programme was as exciting as the book. ☐

I was "glued" to the screen. ☐

Did the film or programme have the same pace as the book?
Award it a score out of ten by colouring the boxes.

| 1 | 2 | 3 | 4 | 5 | 6 | 7 | 8 | 9 | 10 |

Could the film or programme have been improved? If so, how?

....

....

....

Do you think the film or programme was better than the book? If so, how?

....

....

....

Which of these have you read and seen?
Did you enjoy them?
Did the film or programme match the book?
Complete this chart.

	Bookshop		Box office		
Title	**Read** ✓or ✗	**Enjoyed** ✓or ✗	**Seen** ✓or ✗	**Enjoyed** ✓or ✗	**Match**
101 Dalmatians by Dodie Smith					/10
The Sheep Pig by Dick King-Smith					/10
Moondial by Helen Cresswell					/10
The Home Farm Twins by Jenny Oldfield					/10
The Borrowers by Mary Norton					/10
The Lion, the Witch and the Wardrobe by C.S. Lewis					/10
Harry Potter and the Philosopher's Stone by J.K. Rowling					/10
Other					/10

Excellent!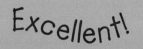

Be a reporter!

You are a top newspaper reporter, writing for your own age group.

Make sure that your reports always:
- have an introduction
- have a clear sequence of information
- present the facts clearly, and give evidence for them
- use language to suit the reader and the subject
- use photographs or illustrations where appropriate

Write a report about one of the following:

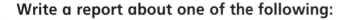

The latest sports equipment | A new interest | A new book or CD | An adventure holiday

Headline

by our features reporter

....

Photograph

....
....
....
....
....
....
....
....
....
....

Help your child to plan his report, referring to the criteria at the top of the page, and make sure that it is factual. Show him how to write in two columns.

Look at a variety of newspapers together, contrasting the sensational and biased reporting in some of the tabloids with more balanced writing.

Good work!

You have mail!

funfox.com

E-mail messages are usually short and snappy.
Write some e-mail messages to people you know.
Begin with an e-mail address and a brief description of the subject of the message.

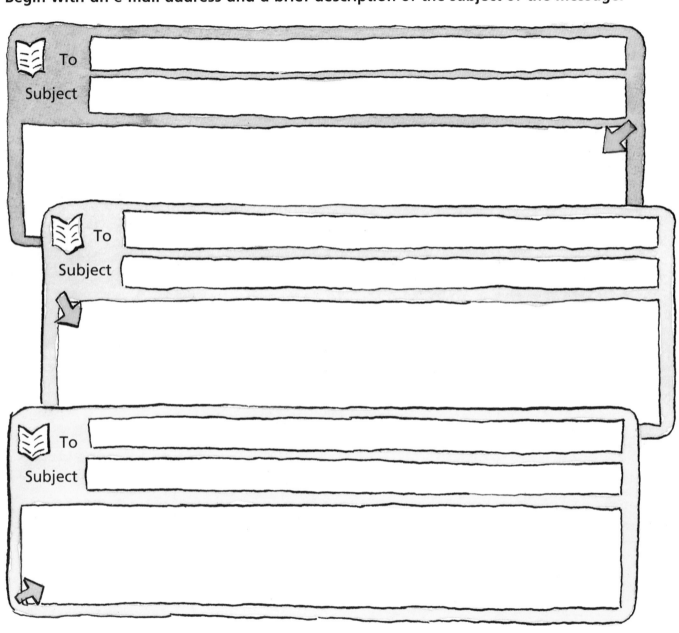

To

Subject

To

Subject

To

Subject

Make up e-mail addresses for yourself and a friend.

....

Invent brief, amusing e-mail addresses together, and make a collection of real ones. Let your child have access to a computer if possible, so that he can send and receive some real e-mails.

Wonderful! ★

Let's find out

If you can find information quickly you can learn more!

You can find information in books,
in CD-Roms and on the Internet.
You need to read quickly and efficiently,
so ask yourself:

- what you want to find out
- where to find the information
- how to read it

What is the Milky Way?

I'll look under "space" or "planets".

I'll skim and scan, and then dive deep!

1 Skim
Read the passage fast to get a feel for it.

2 Scan
Look over the passage quickly, marking key facts.

3 Dive deep
Read the passage slowly, concentrating on its meaning.

4 Make notes and ask questions
Read the passage twice, making notes and writing down any questions.

To sum up ...

1 Skim

2 Scan

3 Dive deep

4 Make notes and ask questions

Let your child practise 'skimming and scanning' and 'diving deep', using short pieces of information text. Have a short quiz to see how well she can remember the facts.

Now try out your skills on this passage!

The Milky Way

Have you heard of the Milky Way? It's a huge, swirling galaxy.

There are about 500,000 stars in the Milky Way, and to fly from Earth to the edge, even in the fastest spacecraft, would take thousands of years. It is an unimaginably huge structure, shaped rather like a Catherine wheel. The Milky Way spins in space, and the stars move round (orbit) its centre.

Our tiny planet Earth orbits our Sun, which is just one of these stars (about two-thirds of the way from the centre of the Milky Way to the edge). Earth spins on its own axis, too. It spins once to complete what we call a day, and it takes 365 days to orbit the Sun.

From any position on Earth we can see from the centre to the edge of the Milky Way with the naked eye. The view from the Southern Hemisphere (the "bottom half" of the world) is best. From the Northern Hemisphere we can see a milky streak of light that is the edge of the galaxy, but with binoculars this streak can be seen as thousands upon thousands of tiny stars, each called a sun.

There are other galaxies in space, too. We don't know how many, but we know that there are four types: the spiral (like the Milky Way), the elliptical, the barred and the irregular, all whirling in the vast emptiness of space. What we are certain of is that there are more stars than we could ever imagine.

Notes

Questions

Let your child use highlighter pens to mark or underline key facts in the passage.

Help her to formulate some questions (e.g. *What do the other galaxies look like?*), and let her have access to non-fiction books on the subject.

Brilliant!

What is it like?

I'm **as cool as a cucumber**!

A **simile** describes something by comparing it to something else.

Your face is **like a beetroot**!

You're **as sharp as a razor**!

1 **Complete these similes.**

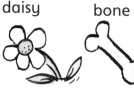
daisy

bone

rain

dove

barrel

toast

pin

March Hare

as warm as ....

as right as ....

as mad as a ....

as fresh as a ....

as dry as a ....

as clean as a new ....

as round as a ....

as gentle as a ....

2 **Invent similes to describe two of your friends.**

.... is as .... as a ....

.... is as .... as a ....

3 **Now invent similes to describe these.**

A cross parent   ....

A new game   ....

An awful meal   ....

A silly film   ....

Make a collection of similes together, and see if you can find any which are particular to your region. Older friends and relatives may know some.

Find a simile for each member of the family (e.g. *Tom is as fit as a fiddle!*)

A metaphor describes something by saying it is something else.

You rat!

Me?

4 **Underline the similes in blue and the metaphors in red.**

a The wind was a torrent of darkness
   among the gusty trees,
The moon was a ghostly galleon
   tossed upon cloudy seas,
The road was a ribbon of moonlight
   over the purple moor,
And the Highwayman came riding …
   riding … riding …
The Highwayman came riding,
   up to the old inn-door.

   From "The Highwayman" by Alfred Noyes

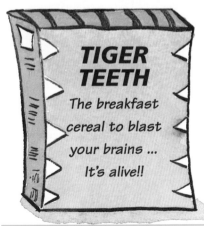

b *The dungeon door clanged, sounding like a giant bell. It echoed, laughing, along the passages of the castle. Their candle flame suddenly died, and spread a blanket of night over the children. They stretched out their hands like blind people. Panic took hold of Sarah, and she screamed. The air vibrated with the sound.*

5 **Invent a metaphor to complete each of these sentences.**

My best friend is a ....   I am a ....

My dad can ....   I can ....

6 **Adverts often use metaphors.**
   Use a metaphor for the name of this drink, and three metaphors to describe it.

TIGER TEETH
*The breakfast cereal to blast your brains …
It's alive!!*

See if your child can spot any metaphors in television advertisements.

Find a metaphor for each member of the family (e.g. *Sam is a walking encyclopaedia!*)

Brainbox!

Thinking about poems

Kenning writer,
Beast fighter,
Field roamer,
Good homer
Long walker,
Fast talker,
I'm Finn Fox!

Read the poems on these two pages, and answer the questions.

A What is a million?

The blades of grass growing
on your back lawn.
The people you've met
since the day you were born.

The age of a fossil
you found by the sea.
The years it would take you
to reach Octran Three.

The water drops needed
to fill the fish pool.
The words you have read
since you started school.

By Wes Magee

B

He sat there watching her and smiled.
He thought, I'm going to eat this child.
Compared with her old Grandmama,
She's going to taste like caviare.

*Then Little Red Riding Hood said, "But Grandma,
what a lovely great big furry coat you have on."*

"That's wrong!" cried the wolf. "Have you forgot
To tell me what BIG TEETH I've got?
Ah well, no matter what you say,
I'm going to eat you anyway."

The small girl smiles. One eyelid flickers.
She whips a pistol from her knickers.
She aims it at the creature's head,
And BANG BANG BANG, she shoots him dead.

A few weeks later, in the wood,
I came across Miss Riding Hood.
But what a change! No cloak of red,
No silly hood upon her head.

She said, "Hello, and do please note
My lovely furry WOLFSKIN COAT."

From *Little Red Riding Hood and the Wolf*
by Roald Dahl

C "F"

*Frightful Friday,
fairly foggy,
forest freezing -
frozen Froggie.*

*Froggie feels
feet freeze;
fancies food -
follows fleas.*

*Fleas frightened,
fleas flee,
fleas fast -
fleas free.*

*Freezing Friday,
fairly foggy,
forest freezing -
fed-up Froggie.*

By Michael Rosen

1 Which poem makes you think deeply (is philosophical)? ☐

2 Which poem do you find funny? ☐

3 Which is a narrative (story) poem? ☐

4 Which poem do you like best? ☐

Give the reason. ....

....

Read each poem aloud, and discuss your reactions.

Talk about the questions before your child writes the answers,
and encourage her to find more poems in her favourite style.

The Charge of the Light Brigade

Half a league, half a league,
Half a league onward,
All in the valley of Death
   Rode the six hundred.
"Forward the Light Brigade!
Charge for the guns!" he said:
Into the valley of Death
   Rode the six hundred.

"Forward the Light Brigade!"
Was there a man dismayed?
Not though the soldier knew
   Someone had blundered:
Theirs not to make reply,
Theirs not to reason why,
Theirs but to do and die:
Into the valley of Death
   Rode the six hundred.

Cannon to the right of them,
Cannon to the left of them,
Cannon in front of them
   Volleyed and thundered;
Stormed at with shot and shell,
Boldly they rode and well,
Into the jaws of Death,
Into the mouth of Hell
   Rode the six hundred.

By Alfred Lord Tennyson

5 In this war poem, who are the six hundred?

....

6 Which word tells you that they are on horses?

....

7 Where were the cannon?

....

8 Which three metaphors tell the reader that the Light Brigade won't survive?

....

9 Which three lines tell the reader that they had to obey orders whatever happened?

....

....

10 Which line in the third verse tells you that they were brave?

....

11 What did you think of this poem?

....

Knowing the background to this poem may make the content more meaningful for your child. It was written in 1854, to celebrate a memorable but misguided action by a British cavalry unit in the Crimean War.

Contrast the contemporary poems on page 24 with this nineteenth century example.

....

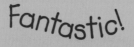

Fantastic!

All about you

The term **curriculum vitae** is Latin for **course of life**.

The abbreviation **CV** stands for **curriculum vitae**.
A CV is a summary of your career at school (or work).
You can show it when you are applying for a new school (or job).

1 **Choose a type of secondary school, and write a CV for yourself.**

A sports academy

An art school

A music college

The local comprehensive

A dance academy

An equestrian college

A drama school

I will apply to ....

Name .... **Age** .... **D.O.B.** ....

Boy/girl .... **Address** ....

Schools attended	**Certificates and awards**
Hobbies and interests	**Personal qualities**
Expected exam results	

You may have written a CV for your child's transfer to secondary school. If not, this is a good time for him to take stock, appraising his skills and planning for the future.

2 Now write a paragraph or two outlining your future plans and giving your reasons for choosing that type of school.

Think carefully!

Additional information

(CV cont.)

Signed ....

You can make up some of the information here!

3 Think of a story character and write a CV for him or her.

Name .... Age .... D.O.B. ....

Male/female .... Address ....

Schools attended

Certificates and awards

Hobbies and interests

Personal qualities

Additional information

Discuss Question 2, helping your child to formulate his reasons for attending a particular school, and to name personal qualities which he can offer the school.

Very interesting!

27

Be a copywriter!

An **advertisement** is a presentation which has been designed to **persuade** people to buy something.
It may be spoken or printed.
It may include pictures.

A good advertisement:

- uses superlatives (e.g. biggest)
- grabs your attention
- uses clear, simple language
- makes the product look interesting
- may use scientific or emotional language
- speaks directly to YOU

1 **Write each persuasive word or phrase under the correct heading.**

State of the art
GLAMOROUS
Latest
WONDERFUL
YOU OWE IT
TO THEM
*Memories are made
of this …*

Quality
Every mum knows
YOU can't do
without
Do you want a
LOOK
BIGGEST
Sale

Proven
Last few
Buy now
Free
Wow
Blue Cross
Tests show
Best

Researched in
our labs
One left
**Lifetime's
experience**
NEED
According to
scientists

Grabs your attention	Uses scientific language	Uses emotional language	Uses superlatives	Uses clear, simple language	Speaks directly to you

Some of the phrases could go under more than one heading.

Try to spot these examples of persuasive language in advertisements and on packaging. Look at full-page advertisements in glossy magazines, and compare the language with that used in classified advertisements in newspapers.

You too can write the finest, the best, the BIGGEST ad ever!

2 **Now design three magazine advertisements.**
Use different styles of lettering, and add colourful pictures.

A new toy for children under 7

A book for 10–15 year-olds

Clothing or a CD for 10–15 year-olds

These advertisements could be aimed directly at children or at their parents.

Look at the language used on the back covers of books (blurbs, reviewers' comments, awards the book has won).

Exciting!

Skills test

Read this passage from *Warrior Scarlet*, the story of a boy in Iron Age Britain.

He held the puppy up, swinging a little from its loose scruff; he laughed as it tried from an arm's length away to lick his nose, and knew that the perfect moment, the best moment of all, had come.

"I have bought my hound!" he said to the world at large. "I have paid the price for him, and he is mine! I shall call him Whitethroat!"

"So, that is a good name," Talore said. "And now it is time to be going home."

Drem looked up from the puppy. "I shall need to leave my spear here until tomorrow," he said, "so that I can carry the cub."

"Assuredly," Talore nodded. "His legs are but two moons old, and the way will be over-long for them; yet first make him follow you a little. It is so that he will understand that he is your hound, to follow at your heel."

Drem looked at the hunter doubtfully for a moment, then squatted down and set the puppy on its legs. "Will he come, do you think?"

"Call him and see."

Drem got up and took a step backward. "Hi! Whitethroat, come!"

The puppy continued to sit on its haunches. It was too small as yet to prick its ears, but it fluttered them, gazing up at Drem with the air of one trying to understand what he would have it do. Drem drew another step towards the doorway.

"Come! We go home now, brother."

The puppy whimpered and made a small thrusting motion towards him. Aware that everyone in the house-place was watching him, Drem took yet another backward step. He was almost at the threshold now.

"Whitethroat – here!" His throat ached with urgency, and the words came hoarse.

He whistled a two-note call that he had never thought of before, but that seemed to come to him now as the proper call between him and Whitethroat. The small, brindled half-wolf cub got up, sneezed, shook itself and waddled towards him, its stomach brushing the ferny ground. Once it hesitated, and looked back at Fand, its mother, with an air of uncertainty, and then padded forward again. And Drem knew that he had been wrong in thinking that the moment when he picked it out from the litter had been the best moment of all.

From *Warrior Scarlet* by Rosemary Sutcliff

I'm going to read the rest of this book. Are you?

Write a blurb to advertise *Warrior Scarlet*, to go on its back cover.

Write a review praising the author's style.

Now write a very critical review.

Finally, write your own review, giving your real opinion of the passage.

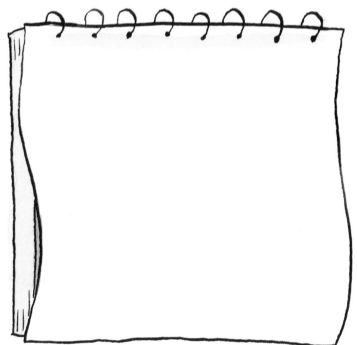

You could write a review of a different book for your child to use as a model.

Help him to appraise his 'blurb' and his reviews. What did he find difficult? Did he understand the passage? Did he find it easy to formulate his opinions?

Well done!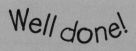

Answers

Pages 2-3
1-6
Discuss the questions, and encourage thoughtful, honest answers.

Pages 4-6
1
He is talking to himself.
Possible quotations:
... to shut himself in the kitchen to finish preparing dinner ...
... could not cook unless he had absolute privacy and silence ...
... promised himself as he turned down the oven ...
2
He is really concentrating on the cooking. We know this because he talks about his cooking in great detail, whereas his comments about the dog are much briefer.
3
present, future
4
Preventing further suffering by putting the dog to sleep.
5
They are trying to push him through the catflap.
6
Sun Dance says, "When is it dinner time?"
7
He beats his head against the kitchen wall.
8
She tells Beany to shut Old Blanket in the porch and give him some sausages; she tells Sun Dance to get his father a drink of whisky; she goes to rescue the dinner.
9 -14
free choice
Look for answers which are written in complete sentences and give reasons based on the text.

Page 7
1-2
Discuss the questions and encourage thoughtful answers.

Pages 8-9
1
Make sure that your child follows the words in the poem closely when she writes the alternating speeches for the teacher and Graham. The last speech should come from Jonathan. Look for interesting, appropriate stage directions and prompts.

2
The rewritten text should follow the conventions of a playscript (see page 8) and include some of the actions as prompts (e.g. Elspeth: {walking into the room and grinning} There you are!)

Pages 10-15
Look for interesting, well structured ideas when your child is planning a story and inventing the characters. When he or she is trying out different writing styles, encourage fluent writing and correct punctuation.

Pages 16-17
Look for thoughtful answers based on the book and the film or programme.

Page 18
Look for fluent, focused, factual writing which keeps to the criteria given.

Page 19
The messages should be brief and to the point.

Pages 20-21
Look for brief notes which are based on key words, and carefully considered questions based on the passage.

Pages 22-23
1
as warm as toast
as right as rain
as mad as a March Hare
as fresh as a daisy
as dry as a bone
as clean as a new pin
as round as a barrel
as gentle as a dove
2-3
free choice
Make sure your child has used the construction as ... as a ..., or like a ... when answering Question 3.
4
Similes: like a giant bell (b)
like blind people (b)
Metaphors: the wind was a torrent of darkness among the gusty trees (a)
the moon was a ghostly galleon tossed upon cloudy seas (a)
the road was a ribbon of moonlight over the purple moor (a)
it echoed, laughing (b)

their candle flame suddenly died ... spread a blanket of night (b)
panic took hold of Sarah (b)
5-6
free choice

Pages 24-25
1 A **2** B or C **3** B **4** *free choice*
5
the Light Brigade
6
rode
7
to the right of them, to the left of them, in front of them
8
the valley of Death
the jaws of Death
the mouth of Hell
9
Theirs not to make reply
Theirs not to reason why
Theirs but to do and die
10
Boldly they rode and well
11
free choice

Pages 26-27
1
Look for a detailed, positive summary of your child's achievements, interests and personality.
2
Look for thoughtful, interesting views.
3
Look for appropriate information expressed in suitable language.

Pages 28-29
1
Discuss the answers; some of the phrases could go under more than one heading.
2
Look for attractive, well planned advertisements which make good use of colour, pictures, special lettering and some of the slogans from page 28. Make sure the wording uses suitable language for the target age groups (or their parents).

Pages 30-31
The reviews should be concise but detailed, showing understanding of the content and style of the text. Look for correct grammar, punctuation and spelling, and neat handwriting.